Diary of Dogsbody

© 1994 David Downe

All rights reserved. No reproduction, copy or transmission of this publication may be made without written permission. No paragraph or illustration of this publication may be reproduced, copied or transmitted save with written permission from Owl Press or in accordance with the provisions of the Copyright, designs and Patents Act 1988. Any person who does any unauthorised act in relation to this publication may be liable to criminal prosecution and civil claims for damages.

Published by Owl Press, P.O. Box 315 Downton, Salisbury, Wiltshire. SP5 3YE. 1994
Printed in the UK by BPC Wheatons Ltd, Exeter.

British Library Cataloguing - in - Publication data. A catalogue record for this book is available from the British Library.

Publisher's ISBN: 1 898052 20 4

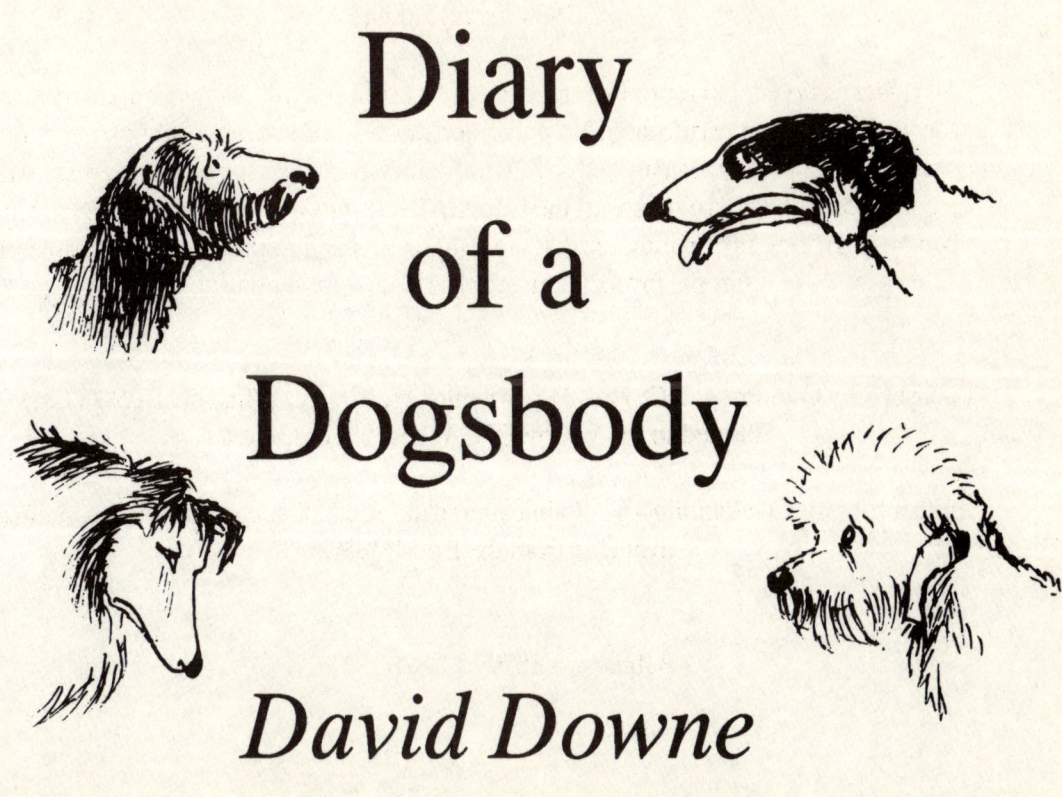

Diary of a Dogsbody

David Downe

About The Author
David Downe

    David Downe was born, chuckling, during the depression of 1931 and is still smiling. In between times he was educated at St Edwards Oxford and the Royal Military Academy Sandhurst. He was commissioned in 1951, 'retired' in 1968 and became variously thereafter, unemployed for one blissful year, a freelance cartoonist in Fleet Street and ultimately Director of the West Midlands Museum Service. After living like a gypsy with no caravan, he and his family have settled near Worcester.

    During his career as a cartoonist he has contributed to the cartoon columns of most of the popular and less popular press as well as to specialist collections. Now retired from the museum service, he has returned to drawing cartoons. In 1993 he wrote and illustrated *A Regimental Mess*, a collection which explores the prospects for redundancy and resettlement in the Services. He is currently working on a new collection called *Collecting Antics*, with writer Les Lilley, which looks at the world of antiques, bric-a-brac and car boot sales, where true collectors satisfy their addiction for finding "The Big Bargain".

"for Scrumpy, Muffin and Pippin, our three Dandie Dinmonts."

Time for a Doggone Dog

I considered getting a dog. Or rather I felt that I had reached the age and position in life that demanded that I should get a dog. What, I wondered, would it be like?

What use would it be to me?

What brand would suit me best?

I was told that a dog was a noble animal, supposedly 'man's best friend'. As far as I could see, from my every day encounters with the canine world, dogs were a constant source of companionship, embarrassment and irritation. Dogs could be:-

Proud,
Humble,
Obedient,
And a bloody nuisance.
Frustrating,
Loyal in adversity,
Insufferable companions who disappear for hours just as you want to go home.

A dog can sponge or hunt, hate or mate, guard you, guide you, keep you, feed you, trip you up, win prizes, lose money, collect the paper, leave nasty things on the carpet and just as you make your last journey to the great kennel in the sky a dog will pee on your headstone for old time's sake.

There was much more to entering this doggy world than I had first thought. What a choice of breeds and types, shapes and sizes. There were brands that would fit into palaces, country houses, suburban-semis, bungalows, villas or even cardboard boxes; there was a dog for every human condition.

I could choose a St Bernard, who would rescue me, even if he was a trifle large. Or a Bulldog to guard me, even if he was rather fierce. Then there was a Sheepdog, who could look after and control my livestock but might be a shade too clever to live with. An Alsatian perhaps, who could solve crimes but who might frighten my more nervous friends.

Poodles and Petues, Dandie Dinmonts and Dachshunds, Whippets and Wolfhounds, Spaniels and Salukis, Borzois, Afghans, Spaniels, Terriers, Samoyeds, Bassets and others I could mention.

All in all there seemed to be an inexhaustible supply of breeds who, like boxes of chocolates, made selection difficult by having hard and soft centres.

In the event I chose a very undistinguished Mongrel.

Man's best friend!

A constant source of companionship

"I take it he's just like one of the family Judge?"

Embarrassment

"My God have you been playing 'Pop the football' with that kid next door again?!"

And yet more embarrassment

"I suppose mating is a bit of a nostalgia trip for him nowadays."

A source of irritation

"Blasted fellar's forgotten his horn and thinks all you have to do is shout 'Heel'!"

A dog can be.....frustrating

"It's not so much that he has his tongue stuck in a milk bottle, but it always has to happen on a Monday morning."

A dog can.....hate

"I take it you've heard of the expression - Dog eat dog?"

A dog can.....mate

Collect your paper

"Now, hold it gently in your mouth like this, taking care not to wet the crossword."

Leave nasty things on your carpet

Your last journey to the kennel in the sky

Dogs have insinuated themselves into our language. There are dog ends.....

.....and dogs in a manger

"I take it he feels 'silagistically' challenged?"

Doggerel

"He's not <u>that</u> clever - he can't think of a last line."

Dog days

"Hang on Hector - there's no reason for you to go putting yourself down!"

Doggy bags

"Honestly, it's just a little doggy bag from my last meal in Paris."

Even a doge of Venice

"*Right Georgio - that post over there will do us nicely.*"

Dogs that come in all shapes and sizes

"Do you remember what a sweet cuddly little mongrel puppy she was when she first arrived?"

A different brand of dog for every human condition

"She's become an ardent Bitchist and now she will only cock her leg."

The St Bernard

"....Cheers! You got here at last!"

The bulldog

The sheepdog

"OK I've got 'em penned up here - where do you want me next?"

An alsatian to guard you

The pointer

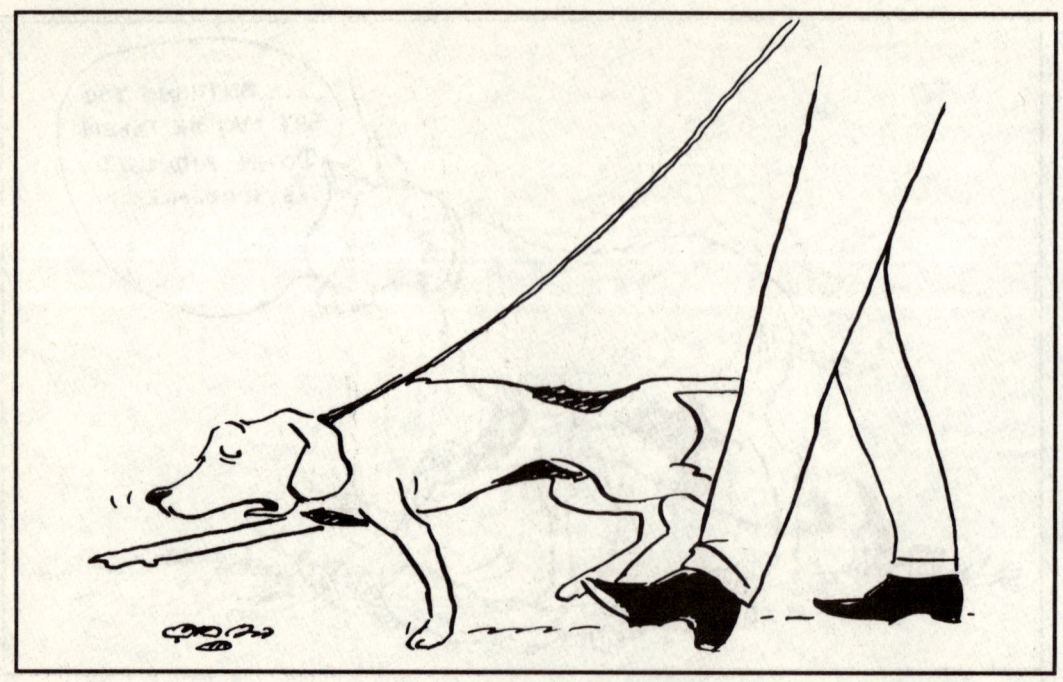

"...that's Mrs Smith over there.....look at that dreadful window display.....watch out dog mess ahead.....keep right of the ditch.....just look at that!"

The gun dog

"This is the fourth bra and pants this season."

A sniffer dog

A husky

"They say that it's them and not Ranulf Fiennes who should haul sleds around Antarctica."

A town dog

"Your sheep have been worrying my dog!!"

A country dog

" - Rabies!! <u>My</u> dogs only catch what I tell them to catch!"

Last but not least.....a mongrel

"He's what you might call a <u>real</u> mongrel's mongrel!"

The Dogsbody Deal

Most people with pedigree dogs check out their bloodlines with considerable care. There are bloodlines that come from as far back as Adam and Eve and the Ark. A Mongrel, on the other hand, is lop-eared, mixed up and invariable ferociously athletic. If your mongrel is like mine, he is in over-drive just seconds after he has risen from his basket and will need to circle the block at least three times before lunch and six times afterwards.

As a new owner I felt that nothing I asked of my new companion would be too much. In return, it was agreed, I should provide food, medical care, a basket and plenty of understanding. I had to grant him soccage and pillage rights on my property, excavation and burial rights within the boundaries of my flower beds and obtain for him the necessary veterinary protection and insurance against rabies, scabies and fathering too many babies (although this last provision was written in more at my behest than his).

Lastly came the vexed question of walks, to be supplied at the rate of at least three a day, in order to cream off the supply of nervous energy which might make it difficult for him to sleep at night. I had a feeling that walking my new found friend would be as difficult and continuous as painting the Forth Bridge.

Next I had to find a name; nothing ordinary like Bonzo, Rover or Patch would do. On the other hand nothing too exotic or fanciful should be employed that would make him feel ashamed or, more to the point, embarrass me when calling for him in public.

When it came down to it there were two sorts of names I could choose from; a kennel name and a pet name. Kennel names are complex and long-winded to reflect a dog's attributes or pedigree or your own vanity. Whatever name I chose it should have the ring of quality about it. Titles like Bratwurst Floppydisc (Dachshund), High Fibre Hurricane (Spaniel), Borderline Lunatic (Rotweiler), Sir Toby Belch (any classical breed with gastronomic problems) or even Maastricht Not B----y Likely (English Setter) seemed rather grand for my new friend.

So I chose a pet name. These can range from the endearing to the eccentric like Crumpet, Hanky Panky and Gervase, or at the other extreme Pissov, (like the particularly memorable Borzoi who patrolled my neighbourhood at the height of the Cold War).

In the event I settled on the name 'Chutney' as I relished the prospect of his company and it was he who would entirely train me.

Mongrels go back to Adam and Eve

"He's gone and pinched my last autumn fig leaf to play with!"

Mongrel ancestry - The Ark

"We can't take every breed so I've bunged in a couple of Mongrels."

Breeding

"I really can't say whether they look like their father or not, I never saw his face."

Sexually harrass bitches

"Litter Lout!"

Act in films

"I'm sure he's a great fan of both of them but no dogs under 2 are allowed in accompanied or not. A rule is a rule."

Sniff explosives and other noxious substances

"Half close your eyes, then sniff slowly from right to left making sure you don't miss the underside of any shelves."

Aggravate the postman

"He's only joined because he's worried about the recent decline in the number of trees."

Provision of food and medical care

"Quick love - pass me the inspection lamp."

Provide him with shelter

The question of walks

"I should warn you that some of his walks are sexually explicit and contain scenes that may shock and disturb you."

Cream off the supply of nervous energy

"You're just going to have to wait until we get home!"

Kennel names

"First, Whiplash Gentleman's relish!...Second, Harmony Hot Water Bottle...Third, Goliath of Gath."

Pet names

"I don't care what your dog is called lady - you don't go shouting 'Mayday' around here!!"

Dogtired and Devoted

Men (and women) have been bitten by dogs through countless ages which makes it surprising that such a bond of friendship should exist between these two such very differing breeds.

As soon as I had adopted my own dog I found that I had acquired an extensive and formidable array of new friends and acquaintances of incredible diversity; policemen and petty crooks, New Age Travellers and fleas, Old Age Pensioners and 'yoofs', hearty breeders and limp wristed salesmen, dustmen and duchesses, doting owners, do-gooders, do-badders, bereaved owners, porcelain collectors, tramps, royalty, unisex barbers, vets, radio personalties and many, many others who all doted, boasted or gave free advice on dogs in general and my own in particular.

I was invited to go to dog shows, take tea and coffee, collect money for the RSPCA, join the Canine Defence League and take my dog to meet other dogs with a view to matrimony (either my own or his).

Chutney and I became inseparable. He slept on my bed, walked with me, ate my food, introduced me to canker, parasites and fleas and was unfaithful only once when he fell temporarily in love with a sympathetic kennel maid who fed him illicit dog biscuits while I was away.

On hot summer days he splashed in rivers and ponds and then shook himself dry next to me. In winter he sat happily by my fireside in the best position and farted with noxious intensity in total contentment.

Vets had a startling effect on him. He could feign illness with a thespian skill, develop fraudulent swellings and retain pills in his mouth for hours on end and then spit them out when he thought no one was looking. He could reject thermometers with one flick of his tail and create anarchy in a surgery or waiting room of assorted patients, scalded cats, poorly parrots and hamstrung hamsters within seconds of entering the door.

We lived like this for twelve tumultuous years sharing everything on the basis of what's yours is mine and what's mine is my own. He loved <u>my</u> sweets, <u>my</u> meat, <u>my</u> puddings, <u>my</u> pastries. He was eternally grateful for his share of <u>my</u> bed and <u>my</u> board. I, on the other hand, never actually managed to acquire his taste or enthusiasm for Tinned Meaty Chunks, Dog Biscuits, dead birds, chewed rats or compost.

As time went on he gradually slowed down matching his pace to mine, in the process he became softer and no longer drank his beer at the Pub from the ash tray but preferred to sip it from a glass. He went off children, long walks and began to creak as he pursued cats and bitches - rather hoping that he would not catch either.

Policemen

"Now let's see...just a faint hint of Dachshund mixed with Kerry Blue and a smidgen of Terrier and a tail that curls slightly if you wet it."

Old age pensioners

"You can chain them both to my zimmer frame - I won't be far away when you get back."

'Yoof

Hearty breeders

"You and I should get together for a spot of mating soon."

Dustmen

"It's OK mate - he always gets in for a quick snack every Thursday."

Tramps

Royalty

Royalty

"I trust we haven't done anything that makes you feel uncomfortable."

Radio personalities

"Now before the next record I have a quick interview with a dog who claims to be the great-great-grandson of the HMV record dog."

Computer experts

Give free advice on dogs in general

"My little Prudence isn't on heat - she's just temporarily thermally extended."

Advice on my own dog in particular

"Why is it always <u>your</u> dog that has to look up ladies' skirts?"

Take my dog to meet other dogs with a view to matrimony

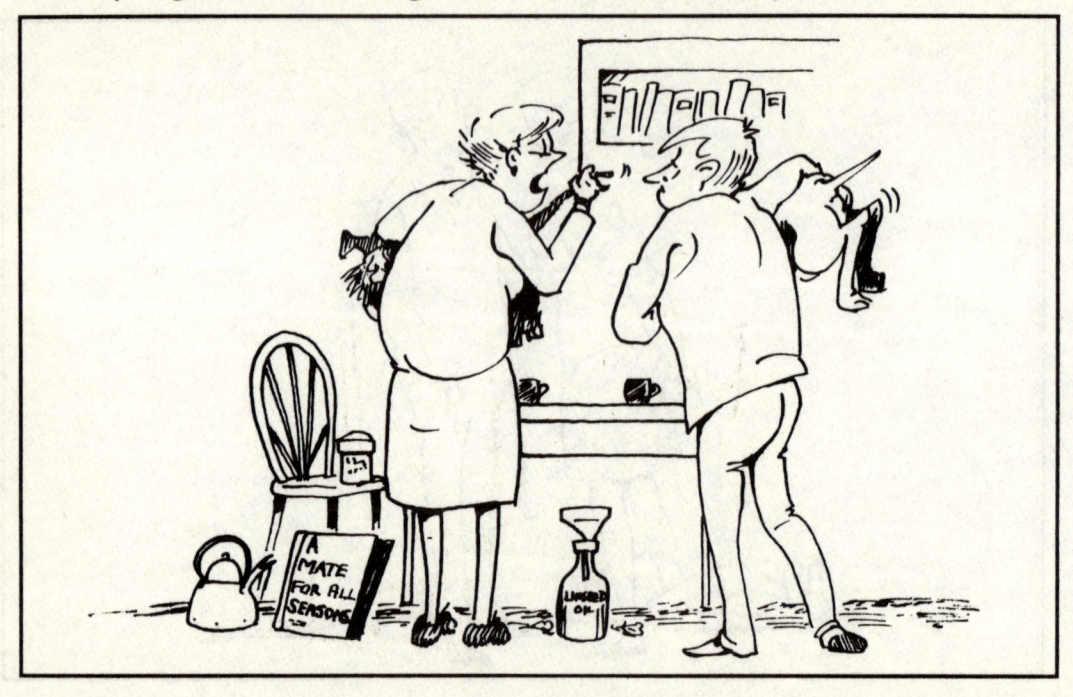

"When I say, 'Go' - remember to aim dead centre and jig around like blazes until I say, 'Stop'."

Chutney and I became inseperable

"I promise there is no one else!"

Walked with me

The intricacies of blowing pills down his throat

"Why does pill taking always turn into such a battle of wills?!"

Outrageous behaviour with other dogs particularly bitches

"Don't worry Mrs Copperfield it's known in the trade as 'Foreplay'!"

Vets had a startling effect on him

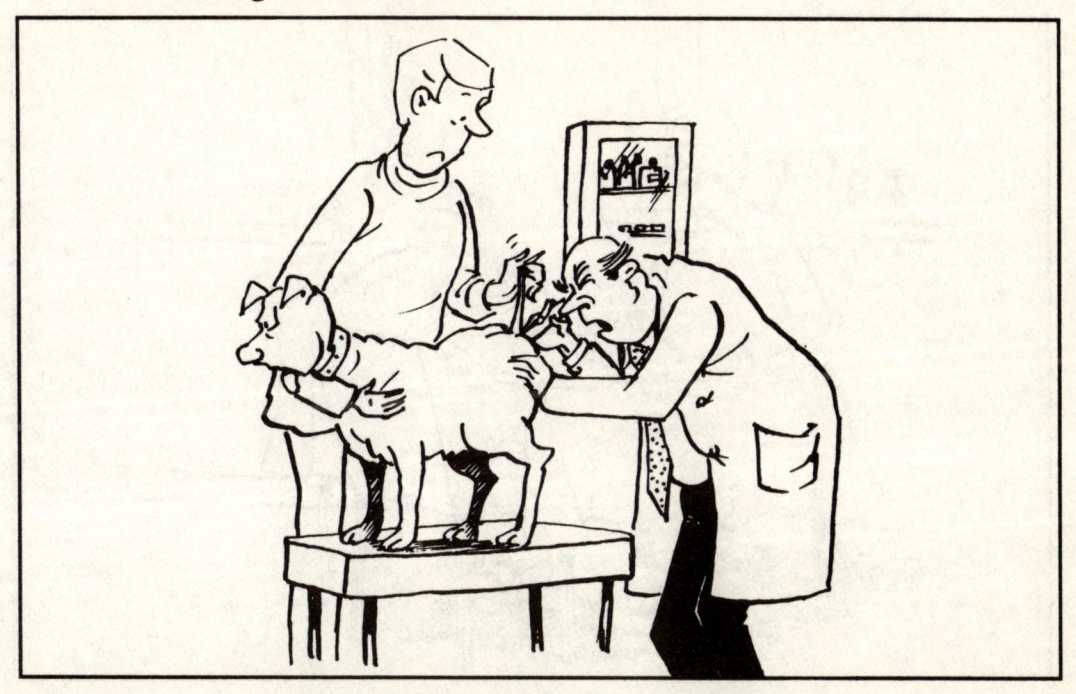

"Well, it looks like his tonsils need seeing to!"

Noxious intensity

"How is it dear that you always manage to achieve that rich aroma of beans, vegetables and herbs when you cook for us?"

Creates anarchy in the surgery or waiting room

"Actually he's a South African Plague Dog."

Music played for him at every birthday

"Politically he appeared to favour the right

He was a very mixed up character

"How long have you been in the bottle bank this time?"

He never complained of the ageing process

Dog-days to the End

The End when it came one bright sunny morning took us both by surprise. He had gone to his basket the previous night after eating his ample snack of choco-drops as usual. The next morning when I came down to let him out for his usual nose around I found that he had already gone to a far more interesting hunting ground. He left a half-eaten biscuit in his basket, the only unfinished business I could recall in a lifetime of fulfilled eating.

Everyone was very sympathetic and helpful.

"Why don't you get another dog?" they suggested. "Another companion. A successor."

But I refused. It wouldn't have been right.

I buried him at the bottom of my garden in the shade of the giant compost heap where I knew he would feel at home.

For a long time afterwards I wondered how he was getting on up there. A quick sniff at the Golden Gate and then away to join Sirius -the dog star who according to ancient Egyptians rose with the sun and flooded the Nile. Something well within Chutney's tastes and capacity.

Amongst my books I found this rather fitting epitaph for the faithful friend I mourned,

> 'This tombstone, stranger passing near
> Shows that a little dog lies here.
> Tells how a master's loving hand
> Carved these words and heaped this sand.
> Smile, if you please, but when you die
> Will you be mourned as much as I?'

Ancient Greek Epitaph for a pet dog.

I buried him at the bottom of my garden

"He always loved having his tummy tickled."

I prefer to think of him being up there

"*Of course you could try again as a born again mongrel.*"

Knocking at the Golden Gates

"Here's a copy of our house rules, which you might have a bit of difficulty with - the cats and postmen clauses for instance."